Oz Clarke is one of the world's leading wine experts, known for his phenomenal palate, irreverent style, accurate predictions, and enthusiasm for life in general and wine in particular. He is the author of many award-winning books on wine and his BBC television and radio broadcasts keep audiences spellbound and entertained. Before wine took over his life in 1984, Oz was a full-time actor and singer, appearing in West End hit shows and touring with the Royal Shakespeare Company. He currently presents a series of concerts, Drink to Music!, with the acclaimed Armonico Consort. Oz is also sports mad.

OZ CLARKE'S
WORLD OF WINE

WINES GRAPES VINEYARDS

First published in the United Kingdom
in 2017 by
Pavilion
43 Great Ormond Street,
London WC1N 3HZ

www.pavilionbooks.com
www.ozclarke.com

A CIP catalogue for this book is
available from the British Library.

ISBN 978-1-910904-96-1

10 9 8 7 6 5 4 3 2 1

Printed by Toppan Leefung Printing Ltd,
China
Reproduction by Rival Colour UK

This book can be ordered direct
from the publisher at
www.pavilionbooks.com

*Captions: Pages 2–3 View from Clayridge
Vineyard to Cloudy Bay Barracks Vineyard
in the Upper Omaka Valley, Marlborough,
New Zealand.
Pages 4–5 Sorting harvested Merlot
grapes in the vineyard of Château
Haut-Brion, Pessac-Léognan, Bordeaux,
France.*

For wine recommendations,
special offers and news on Oz's
upcoming books and events visit
www.ozclarke.com and sign
up to the Oz Clarke newsletter.
Follow Oz on Twitter @OzClarke

Contents

About Wine

Sometimes I stop and ask myself: when was the last time I had a glass of bad wine? Not wine that is out of condition, or corked wine, or wine that I've left hanging around in the kitchen for too long – but poor, stale, badly made, unattractive wine? And unless I've been extremely unlucky in the previous month or so, I won't be able to remember. The standard of basic winemaking is now so high that a wine drinker need never taste a wine that is not at very least clean, honest and drinkable. It wasn't like that a generation ago. And then, I sometimes idly try to work out how many different grape varieties from how many different wine regions I've tried during a typical wine-taster's week. At a recent tasting I counted the number of grape varieties contributing to an exciting array of wines. Seventy different grape varieties, from places as familiar as France and Italy and Spain, and as far flung as Tasmania and Brazil, New York and Bolivia. And it wasn't like that a generation ago, either.

For me the thrilling thing about this modern world is that we now have choice – endless choice that gets bigger every year. And with choice, comes excitement, challenge, but also confusion. But that's why this book is here to help you: to make sense of this cornucopia of flavours and delights that extends from the most famous and expensive wines of Bordeaux and Burgundy down to the first nervous offerings of new vineyards from unsung valleys.

We, as wine drinkers, should take some credit for this transformation. If we were not prepared to try new things, to take a bit of risk with unknown areas and unknown grapes – winemakers would neither bother to resurrect old areas and plant new ones, nor bother to spread their activities beyond a few popular grape varieties. If we weren't prepared to be adventurous, wine companies would simply flood us with a sea of Chardonnay, Sauvignon, Cabernet, Merlot and Shiraz/Syrah, gaudy labels and fantasy names bedecking wines that make no attempt to taste different or individual. But you and I would be missing out on so much.

We are in the midst of a revolution in wine that is bringing together the best of the new and the old. Traditionalists are realizing that maybe the old ways are not always the best, that they can learn something from the brash younger generation. And the modernists are quietly laying aside their reliance on cultured yeasts, scientific formulae and refrigerated stainless steel tanks, and listening with respect to the old farmers with their gnarled vines, and their quiet unhurried ways of letting a wine make itself as it will. Yet, with all this hectic change, the eternal truths of what makes wine good and special have never been more evident. Every good winemaker knows that the final limiting factor on wine quality is the quality of the grapes. And every winemaker knows that some regions grow better grapes than others, some areas within those regions are more suitable, some small patches of the very same field are better than others – and some growers care more about their work and will always produce the finest fruit. And I unashamedly admit that I am more excited by the vineyard, by nature's effect on the final flavour of wine, than I am by a winery, however full of state of art gadgets it may be.

If I'm in Côte-Rôtie, I want to climb to the highest point on the slope from whose grapes the juice always runs blackest and sweetest. I want to feel the poor stony soil crumble beneath my feet and touch the twisted, tortured trunk of the vine which each year struggles to survive on this barren slope and ripen its tiny crop. If I'm in Margaux, I want to tread the warm, well-drained gravel outcrops and then step off into the sullen clay swamps nearby and, with this single step, I'll know why the gravel-grown grapes are precious and the clay-clogged ones are not. I want to see the Andes water gushing down into the fertile vineyards of Chile's Maipo Valley. I want to feel the howling mists chill me to the bone in California's Carneros, and then feel the warm winds of New Zealand's Marlborough tugging at my hair. I want it all to make sense.

And I want to take you to the oldest wine regions on earth and the newest. I want to discuss the most common grape varieties and the rarest. I want to talk about styles of wine that have hardly changed for 8,000 years, and about styles that seem to have been invented only yesterday. Fashion does play a big part in wine. A generation ago we lauded the rich, heady exotic Chardonnays of Australia's Hunter Valley or California's Napa. Now we crave the savoury, lean offerings from Australia's Yarra Valley or California's Sonoma Coast. A generation ago we praised the light and often feeble attempts to ape Burgundy which marked out the early Pinot Noirs of Oregon and New Zealand. Now we cheer their self-confident and definitely non-Burgundian Pinot Noirs with far greater conviction.

In this age when change has come faster than ever before in the world of wine, it is certain that within the decade some vineyards now in decline will be fired by a new confidence and popularity; others now considered so chic will be struggling in the tough real world as their first flush of fame dissolves; and yet others, at this moment mere pastureland or rocky mountainside, will become flourishing vineyards producing wines whose flavours may be entirely different to anything yet achieved on this planet. And all of these I want to share with you in this book.

China is now a serious wine-producing nation. These vineyards are near Ximangtong village in the LanCang River Valley, Yunnan Province. They are way up in the Himalayan foothills and despite serious challenges with infrastructure, Yunnan could prove to be China's best vineyard region yet.

The Story of Wine

Wine is as old as civilization – probably older – while the vine itself is rooted deeply in pre-history. There was at least one species, *Vitis sezannesis*, growing in Tertiary time – just a mere 60 million years ago. I don't expect that *sezannesis* ever turned into wine – not on purpose, anyway, but aeons later its descendant *Vitis silvestris* surely did (and still does in Bosnia-Herzegovina, where it is called the Iosnica) and by the Quaternary era – around 8000BC – the European vine, *Vitis vinifera* (from which nearly all the world's wines are now made), had come on the scene.

The metamorphosis of grape into wine was almost certainly a happy accident. Imagine Stone Age people storing their hedgerow harvest of wild grapes, *Vitis silvestris*, in a rocky hollow ... some of the grapes squash, juice oozes out and, in a flush of autumn sunshine, begins to ferment. The result – however unpalatable to today's tutored taste – must have cheered the chill of cave-dwelling and provided a few much-needed laughs at the onset of pre-central heating winter. Similarly, in the houses of ancient Persia, Mesopotamia, Armenia, Babylon ... the occasional jars of raisined grapes, ready for winter eating, would surely have begun unexpectedly to bubble and froth and magic themselves into a sweet, heady drink. From such haphazard beginnings, wine evolved into an adjunct of civilization: the Georgians were probably at it around 6000BC. Ancient paintings and sculptures show that both Egypt and China were making and drinking it around 3000BC, but it was really the Greeks who first developed viticulture on a commercial scale and turned vinification into a craft. Their wines tended to be so richly concentrated that they were normally drunk diluted: two parts wine to five of water. And they were syrupy sweet – yet with a sting of salt or a reek of resin, cadged from casks washed out in sea-water or from amphoras lined with pitch-pine. Through their trading travels, the Greeks spread their vine-and-wine knowledge around the Mediterranean and were particularly influential in Italy – to the benefit of the world's wine-drinkers ever since.

A 3rd-century AD mosaic from Roman Spain showing treading grapes in a shallow trough or lagar. *Some Spanish vineyards still use them.*

THE ROMANS

By the middle of the 1st century BC, vineyards criss-crossed the Italian landscape from southernmost Sicily to the Alpine foothills and wine was both an everyday beverage and major export. More importantly, as the Empire gained ground, so did the grape: in all their newly won territories, the Romans established vineyards – climate permitting (and even if it didn't look too promising they persevered, as in the Mosel, where they used straw fires, between the vines, to combat autumn frosts). Today, Europe's traditional wine regions – Bordeaux and Burgundy, Rioja and Rhine, Loire and Languedoc – can all claim to have had Roman foundations.

Most of Rome's wine – whether made at home or in the provinces – was a somewhat plebeian tipple: tart and tough, for quaffing young before it turned to vinegar. Often its taste was softened by the addition of honey, herbs or spices – which also acted as preservatives. But not the top-notch wines. These, we must suppose, were noble creations, aged for a decade or more: the legendary Falernian – according to Pliny, so fiery it would catch light from a spark – reached its prime at 20 years yet would happily survive 100. The Romans' ability to age wine – primarily in earthenware amphoras (sealed with pitch or plaster) but later in barrels – represented a significant development in winemaking. But it was short-lived, doomed to disappear with the Empire.

Since the art of amphora-making was lost and wine could no longer be matured – barrels were mostly for transport – quality suffered. But that aside, the Dark Ages were not as murky, in wine terms, as they might have been. In fact, the thrusting barbarians – ever thirsty – not only maintained existing vineyards but also extended them, as in Burgundy where Germanic settlers cleared the forests and replanted with vines. But throughout medieval times, the guardian of Western culture and civilization – Rome's legacy – was the Church; so, for 1,000 years, Europe's wine heritage was largely nurtured by the monasteries. They were expert agriculturalists able to study and develop vine and wine sciences; they were also powerful landowners, whose expansionist policies often involved acquiring established vineyards or planting new ones. The monks produced wine for sacramental purposes, for their own use – fairly frugal in most orders – but primarily for sale; along with other farm produce, it was a major source of income. In the absence of storage know-how, the wines themselves were mostly light and fresh – ripe for quick consumption. At that time, Burgundy was prized for drinking within the year and Bordeaux considered the better for being younger – the exact opposite of today.

WINE TIMELINE

6000 BC It looks as though the first wine was made in Georgia – 8,000 years ago.

2000–146 BC Wine culture really got moving with the Greeks – and their wine god Dionysus.

300 BC–AD 200 Most of Europe's greatest vineyard regions were established by the Romans.

1100s–1200s Without the monasteries wine culture might have died in the Dark Ages.

1154–1453 The birth of claret – England owned Aquitaine (South-West France) for 300 years and created Bordeaux's wine trade.

1500s–1600s The Germans developed the great Riesling grape during the 16th century.

1587 Sherry (Sack) became popular in England after Sir Francis Drake commandeered the King of Spain's barrels.

1632 You can't successfully transport or age wine in fragile glass. New 'English' glass was strong.

1662 Christopher Merret in London first demonstrated how to make sparkling wine.

1681 Corkscrews – the first reference to a 'steel worm' for extracting corks.

1716 1716 saw the first attempts to legally delimit a wine area – in Chianti.

1740s The first airtight corks meant that wine could now be successfully aged in bottle.

1740s Modern wine bottles had straight sides so that they could be 'laid down' to age.

1801 Chaptal, Napoleon's Interior Minister, first gave grape-growing and winemaking a scientific base in his famous Traité.

1843 Barolo is often thought of as Italy's greatest wine, but it only began being made in 1843.

1855 A classification of Bordeaux red and sweet wines and still in use today.

1855–1870s The concept of château – the development of the idea of single vineyards calling themselves 'château' or 'castle'.

1857–1860s Louis Pasteur explained the roles of yeast in wine fermentation and of oxygen in wine spoilage.

1860 Wine labels – until 1860 wine bottles didn't have labels because glue and suitable paper were not available.

1860 Murrieta and Riscal – the great Rioja wine region came to life with the establishment of these two companies.

1863 Phylloxera – a devastating infestation by an aphid that eventually attacked most of the world's vines.

1920–1933 Prohibition, the Great Experiment – actually, the Great Failure – in trying to stop Americans drinking alcohol.

1924 Bottling wine at the property was the only way to ensure it was genuine. Château Mouton-Rothschild was the first to do it.

1935 Appellation Contrôlée – France's commendable attempt to stop wine fraud by delimiting wine regions and their permitted grape varieties.

1936 The establishment of Cabernet Sauvignon as Napa Valley's great red wine variety by the Beaulieu winery.

A gradual progression from the bottle simply being a serving vessel (filled from the cask and taken to the table), to its modern, straight-sided manifestation (suitable for aging and for laying on its side).

CORKS AND BOTTLES

The role of the Church declined with the Reformation – at least in northern Europe – but this did not convulse the wine world half as much as the discovery of the usefulness of corks a century later. For the first time since the Roman era, wine could now be stored and aged successfully. Throughout the Middle Ages it had been kept in cask, which presented a dual handicap: first, too long in wood could rob a wine of all its fruit; second, once the cask was broached the wine inevitably deteriorated unless drunk within a few days. The bottle, with its much smaller capacity, solved the former problem by providing a neutral, non-porous material that allowed wine to age in a different, subtler way and removed the latter problem by providing sealed containers of a manageable size for a single session's drinking.

However, the cork-and-bottle revolution wasn't an instant success: bottles were then so bulbous they would only stand upright, which meant the corks eventually dried out and let in air. But, by the mid-1700s, longer, flat-sided bottles were designed which would lie down, their corks kept moist by contact with the wine. Winemaking now took on a new dimension. It became worthwhile for a winemaker to try to excel, wines from distinct plots of land could be compared for their qualities, and the most exciting could be classified and separated from the run-of-the-mill wines. Today's great names of Bordeaux, Burgundy and the Rhine first began to be noticed.

In the early 19th century, Europe seemed one massive vineyard. In Italy eight out of ten people were earning their living from wine and in France there were vast plantings rolling southwards from Paris. And *Vitis vinifera* had emigrated – thanks to explorers, colonists and missionaries. It went to Latin America with the Spaniards, to South Africa with French Huguenots and to Australia with the English ... Could anything halt its triumphal progress?

Yes, phylloxera. Phylloxera is an aphid which feeds on and destroys *vinifera* roots. It came from America in the 1860s and, by the turn of the century, had destroyed most of the world's vineyards. The solution, grafting *vinifera* on to American rootstocks – the phylloxera-resistant *Vitis riparia* – was expensive. The most immediate effect in Europe was that only the best sites were replanted and the total area under vines shrank dramatically.

The end of the 19th century was a pretty fraught time for wine. The phylloxera aphid was relentlessly continuing its devastation of the world's vineyards – it continues to this day. This brought about chaos in a Europe where wine was a very important part of the national economy of many countries. Fraud and counterfeiting of wine became almost universal and this led in the 1930s to the establishment of France's appellation contrôlée laws. There had been efforts to delimit vineyard areas before – Chianti and Portugal's Douro had both done it – but the French laws have been followed and copied around the world in an attempt to guarantee authenticity. Our obsession with authenticity and provenance was born out of the chaos of the first part of the 20th century.

By now science was also making an enormous difference in the winery and in the vineyard. Louis Pasteur had unravelled the secret of yeasts in the 1860s as well as solving the problem of endemic spoilage in wine. Bordeaux, led by Château Mouton-Rothschild in 1924, had led the way in bottling wine at source to improve

quality and to stop it being adulterated. The malolactic fermentation which causes wine to undergo a second fermentation was finally worked out by Émile Peynaud in Bordeaux in the 1950s. Wine schools were becoming very professional centres like Montpellier in France and Geisenheim in Germany.

But the most important influence on wine in the second half of the 20th century was the arrival of the Californians and Australians as major players. They had two highly influential wine schools – Davis in California and Roseworthy in Australia – both of which preached control at all stages – of fermentation temperature, of hygiene, of maturation conditions. Stainless steel tanks became widespread, the use of oak barrels for aging was enthusiastically adopted, indeed the flavour of oak in wine is often now more evident than the flavour of the grape variety, more's the pity. But the New World believed in single variety wines – especially Chardonnay and Cabernet Sauvignon and began labelling their bottles accordingly, simplifying in one stroke the way wines were presented to the public. Californians and Australians also arrived in droves in Europe, partly to learn the secrets of the classic wine regions, but also to import their New World philosophy. The 'Flying Winemaker' – a New World winemaker employed to resuscitate moribund European vineyards and wineries – became a common sight, and transformed the quality of basic wine across Europe.

The result is that sour, faulty wine need hardly ever be drunk by us nowadays. Admittedly there has been an explosion of banal 'branded' wines in the 21st century, but at least they are consistent, and for those who want something more exciting – there has never been a better moment than now to be a wine lover.

1949 Émile Peynaud is credited with ushering in the modern, science-based world of winemaking.

1951 The first vintage of Grange Hermitage, which became Australia's greatest and most famous wine.

1950–1960s The Bordeaux effect – the use of Bordeaux methods and Bordeaux grape varieties spread around the world.

1961 Ukrainian Konstantin Frank established vinifera grape varieties in New York State.

1963 A future without glass – alternative containers for wine. Tetra Briks and wine boxes lead the way.

1964 Gallo's Hearty Burgundy was the first of the mass market table wine brands – and it was good!

1966 Robert Mondavi founded the first new winery in the Napa Valley since Prohibition.

1968 Italy breaks the mould – Sassicaia Cabernet Sauvignon from Tuscany ushers in the modern era in Italy.

1960s–1970s The Burgundy effect – Burgundy's white grape, Chardonnay, spread around the world, followed, more erratically, by the red Pinot Noir.

1970s The development of mass market wine brands worldwide.

1974 The first Beaujolais Nouveau race and the birth of the 'new red wine' craze.

1975 White Zinfandel is actually pink and it's often called 'blush', and it's a little sweet. It all began in 1975.

1976 The Judgment of Paris – the first time that New World wines beat French wines in a famous blind tasting.

1978 Parker Points – Robert Parker began his Wine Advocate, marking wines out of 100.

1979 Opus One – the joint venture in California between Robert Mondavi and Philippe de Rothschild of Mouton-Rothschild.

1980s Varietal labelling – labelling a wine according to its grape variety dramatically simplified understanding wine for consumers.

1983 The first vintage I tasted of Montana's Marlborough Sauvignon Blanc. Its outrageous flavours blew me away.

1987 Flying winemakers – New World winemakers, usually Australian – who transformed the quality of Europe's basic wines.

1980s–1990s International consultants – nowadays most top wineries worldwide employ a consultant, and the top ones work in several continents. This is when it became popular.

1990s Cabernet conquers the world – it is now the most planted variety in the world. This is when it really took off.

1991 Canadian icewine – Canada made itself famous overnight with its extraordinary sweet icewines.

1998 Nyetimber from Sussex in England wins the trophy for the Best Sparkling Wine in the World.

2000s Natural wine – the new century brings an increased interest in completely non-interventionist winemaking.

2000 Screwcaps – The movement to stop cork-tainted wine by using screwcaps kicks off in Australia and New Zealand.

2011 China comes from nowhere to be one of the most important wine-consuming and -producing countries in the world.

2014 Fraud and the trial of Rudy Kurniawan. The counterfeiting of old wine is finally exposed as a serious worldwide problem.

The Modern Picture

A COUPLE OF THOUSAND YEARS AGO, this map of the world of wine would have looked very different, with both winemaking and consumption being highest in the Middle East and the Eastern Mediterranean, and Greece and Italy not far behind. The rest of Western Europe would hardly have registered at all – and the New World hadn't yet been discovered. The adoption of Islam, with its ban on alcohol, by most Middle Eastern and North African countries has meant that, although vineyards still flourish there, hardly any produce wine grapes, and the centre of wine production has shifted to Western Europe, mainly to Italy, France and Spain. But the greatest growth today is in the New World – in South America, South Africa and Australasia – and most recently in China, which now has the second biggest vineyard area in the world. The vineyards outside Europe now account for 35 per cent of the world's total grapes made into wine.

The question is, of course, who is going to drink the stuff? Consumption, which was generally falling in the mid-1990s, is creeping up again, generally outside Europe, but not yet fast enough to keep pace with production. Countries like Argentina, South Africa, France, Italy and Spain make far more wine than the locals will drink, and the current picture worldwide is that 10–20 per cent more wine is made each year than is drunk. There are countries like Britain and Canada that recorded significant year-on-year increases in wine consumption but have eased up; while the USA is now the biggest global consumer of wine, edging ahead of France and Italy, whose consumption continues to drop. But it is the huge population of China that remains the big unknown. If this rapidly developing nation raised its per capita wine consumption to even one-tenth of that of the USA, then no-one need worry further about a global surplus. It's a changing world out there.

At the end of the 20th century, and into the present one, we saw steep declines in European vineyard acreage, often encouraged by national governments and the European Union. Those declines have now stabilized. Production is growing again – in spite of EU policies to control the situation. But let's look at the Spanish region of Castilla-La Mancha as an example of what is actually happening. The region's vineyards used to cover nearly 560,000ha (1,383,700 acres) – around half of all Spain's vineyards. Now that figure is closer to 465,000ha (1,000,000 acres) but if anything the area now produces more wine, not less, and of a significantly higher quality. Partly this is due to planting better grape varieties but they still have 180,000ha (350,000 acres) of the extremely neutral white Airén planted. Mostly it is due to managing the vineyards more efficiently and introducing irrigation, which has been 'sort of' legal here since 1996. The result is that some vineyards can quadruple their yields with no trouble at all. When irrigation becomes legal in southern France and southern Italy (as it surely will) yields will shoot up there, too. It is already being used on an 'ad hoc' or experimental basis.

In the New World, there are no restrictions on planting, and the area under vine is growing fast to meet increasing export demands: Australia had 90,000ha (222,400 acres) in 1997 and now has just over 135,000ha (333,600 acres). The USA has the best part of 400,000ha (1,000,000 acres). Chile's vineyard, having steadily declined since the 1970s, is also on the increase again thanks to successful exports. The decline of the huge vineyard area of Argentina has reversed and South Africa's and New Zealand's vineyard areas are expanding slightly. Add to this the fact that none of the New World countries have regulations restricting irrigation and yields, unlike Europe, and you end up with large-scale production increases.

Indeed, if you look at where vineyard expansion and wine consumption have been most positive, it is in the New World, and in the countries of northern Europe, for whom the wine revolution which began in the 1980s is now a part of everyday life (their tiny vineyards have greatly expanded, too, with some very decent results).

And the wine we are drinking is different. Some of the wines that are most popular now were of no great consequence a generation ago. Prosecco has become phenomenally popular worldwide as a sparkling style, English fizz is now sought after rather than being thought of as a joke, Champagne is reacting to global warming by offering far more single-grower Champagnes now ripe enough to sell unblended. Rosé – and particularly, Rosé de Provence – is no longer regarded as an expensive joke, but as a category making up more than 10 per cent of the world's wine. Sauvignon Blanc has become more popular, while Chardonnay has eased up, but this is largely because the flavour of oak which captivated us a generation ago, particularly when applied to Chardonnay, is now far less popular. Riesling is still not popular, but Pinot Grigio is very popular and Italian whites in general

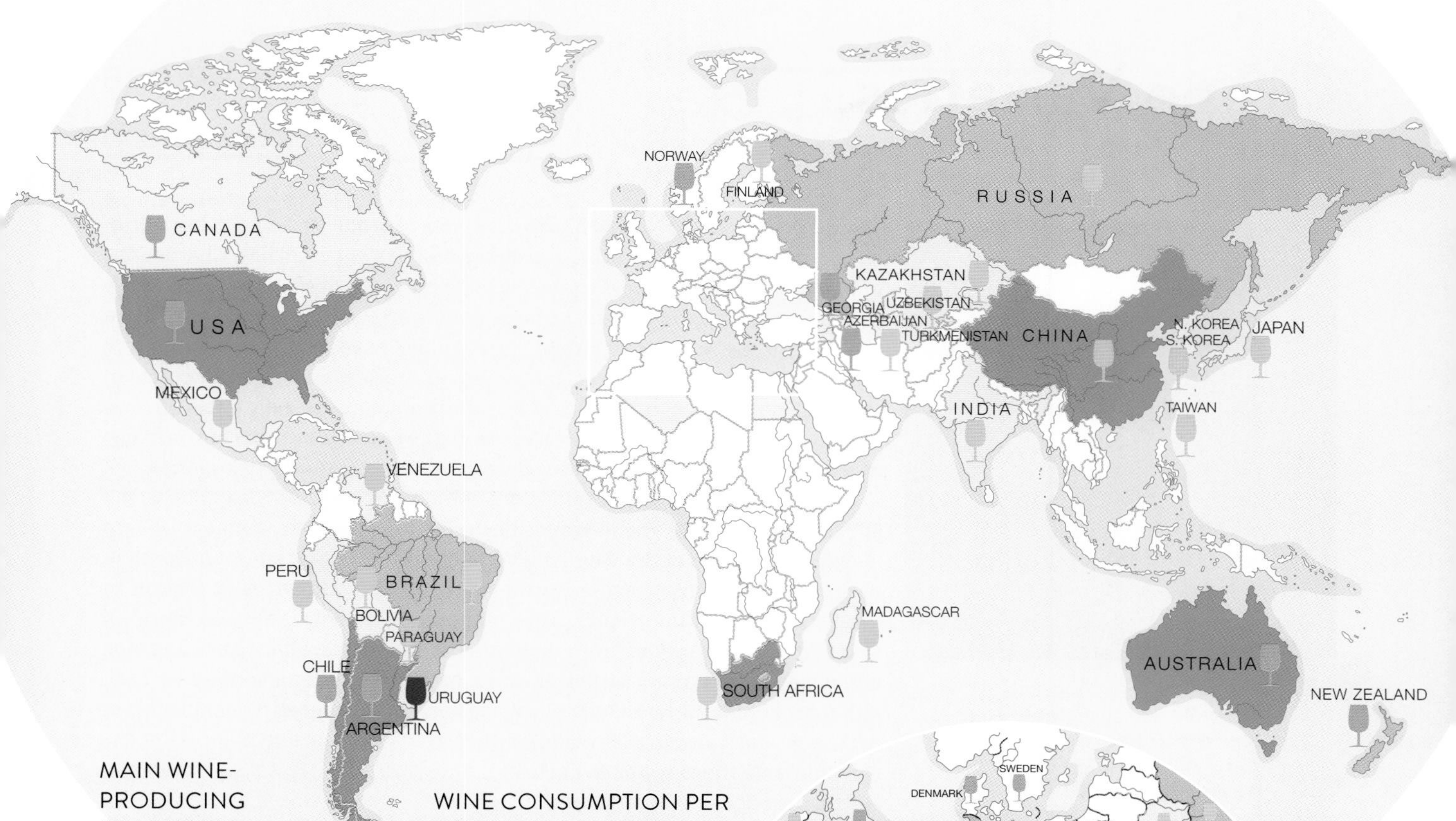

MAIN WINE-PRODUCING COUNTRIES

- Over 10
- 2–10
- Less than 2

(millions of hl per year)

WINE CONSUMPTION PER CAPITA BY COUNTRY

- Over 25
- 10–25
- Less than 10

(litres per capita)

(2014 figures)

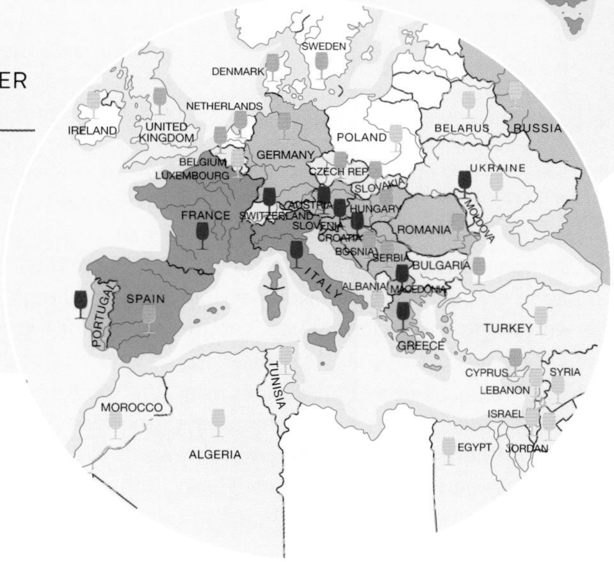

are trendy whereas previously they were regarded as little more than mouthwash.

Cabernet still dominates red wine, but many regions have used Cabernet as a stepping stone that allows them to rediscover their own varieties. Nowadays any country can offer wine made from its own particular grape varieties and find enough people to give it a try. And vineyard regions that had no reputation have developed good niche reputations by concentrating on their specialities: Virginia with its Viognier, New York with its Riesling, Brazil with its Moscatos and fizz, Uruguay with Tannat. And 20 years ago no one would have predicted the worldwide success story that is Argentine Malbec. Pinot Noir was still being talked of as a tricky variety that only Burgundy could grow. Now Chile, Australia, South Africa, Oregon and Canada would dispute that, and California and New Zealand have half a dozen areas each making very individualistic styles.

We have never been more technologically in charge, and quite understandably there has been a reaction – toward natural yeasts, organic and biodynamic vineyards and 'no intervention' wine styles, epitomized by the 'natural' and 'orange' wine movements. And as China finally steps into the wine ring, both as a producer and as a consumer, who knows what effect this will have in the next decade?

Syrah/Shiraz

Chardonnay

Riesling

Sauvignon Blanc

pips it can make raw, lean wine if picked before it is fully ripe, and only the best vineyards regularly excel with it. Blended with Cabernet, it can make a fascinating, stylish bitter-cherry-and-chocolate red wine. It is also important in Emilia-Romagna and elsewhere in Italy.

SYRAH/SHIRAZ

This grape was originally thought of as requiring hot conditions but most of the finest Syrah wines are now coming from areas that are merely warm. Indeed, its home base of the northern Rhône in France is not hot. In hot conditions like Barossa Valley in Australia (where it is called Shiraz) the wines can be rich, dense and succulent, but in cooler areas the flavours are more those of blackberry and raspberry scratched with pepper and scented with flowers. France and Australia are the main producers, but good wines also appear in Canada, California, Chile, Argentina, South Africa, New Zealand and parts of Europe, from warm Spain and Italy to cool Switzerland.

TEMPRANILLO

Tempranillo dominates Spain's quality red wine production – rather too much so, to be frank – and under a variety of names like Tinto Fino in Ribera del Duero, Ull de Llebre in Catalonia and Cencibel in La Mancha and Valdepeñas. But it is most famous as the red wine grape in Rioja. In Portugal it is called Aragonez or Tinto Roriz. It is also doing well in Australia and South America.

ZINFANDEL

The United States imported the first cuttings of this versatile red vine from Europe in the 19th century; they turned out to be the same as the Primitivo variety of southern Italy or Croatia's obscure Crljenak or Tribidrag. 'Zin', however, has become a Californian speciality, used for every sort of wine. But its best expression is as a richly fruity red, full of blackberry or plum flavours. For this, it needs a fairly cool climate and not too much irrigation, since yields can be high. Sugar levels can be high, too, giving a baked, portlike taste. The most intense blackberry and pepper flavours come from old vines. It is not just confined to California, Mexico, Chile, South Africa and Australia also make good Zinfandels.

WHITE GRAPES

CHARDONNAY

The world's favourite white grape is so adaptable it makes everything from light, dry sparkling wine to sweet, botrytized dessert wine, but its dry, oak-aged incarnation, based on the great wines of Burgundy's Côte d'Or, is the best-known style, found from Chile to China, and from California to New South Wales. The wine has such an affinity with new oak (which adds a rich, spicy butteriness) that it can be easy to forget what its varietal flavour is. Unoaked, cool-climate Chardonnay is pale, appley and acidic; these flavours gradually soften towards melon and peach as the climate warms. It is an important component of Champagne and other sparkling wines. In Burgundy, Chardonnay can be a long-lived wine but most examples should be drunk young.

CHENIN BLANC

In France's Loire Valley this versatile grape can produce wines that are dry or sweet, still or sparkling. In both dry and sweet styles, all highly acidic when young, these wines can be put away for years. South Africa also makes a wide variety of Chenin wines, and a little is produced in New Zealand and Western Australia and Argentina.

GEWÜRZTRAMINER

The name means 'spicy Traminer' and that spice is a smell of roses, lychees, sometimes mangoes, often with a dab of face cream and a dusting of ginger. But Gewürztraminer can lack acidity, and needs a cool climate to keep a tendency to high sugar levels in check. At its best in Alsace, followed by New Zealand and Italy's Alto Adige. The vine buds early and is susceptible to frosts. But if it survives these and is affected by noble rot in a warm autumn, superb sweet wines are the result.

MUSCAT BLANC À PETITS GRAINS

The aristocrat of the Muscat family, this low yielder makes intensely grapy wines of more delicacy and fragrance than any of its cousins. It comes in all colours from white to brownish red, and can make delicate scented whites right through to rich, exotic, fortified wines the colour of burnt toffee. It is grown right throughout the Mediterranean, generally making scented sweet wines, but it also makes fizzy Asti in Italy and dry whites in Alto Adige and France's Alsace. It also makes some great fortified wines in Australia.

PINOT GRIS

Famous – or notorious – nowadays as Pinot Grigio, a light, mild, thirst-quencher from northern Italy and Eastern Europe. However, as Pinot Gris in France's Alsace, it makes serious, honeyed golden wines of considerable power. New Zealand also makes some weighty Pinot Gris, but mostly the lighter style is followed, in Romania, Slovenia, Hungary, England and Germany as well as in British Columbia, Oregon, Washington State and (usually as Pinot Grigio) in California and Australia.

RIESLING

Cold-resistant, late-ripening grape that makes thrilling, delicate wines in Germany as fleeting as gossamer and as low as 7.5 per cent in alcohol, as well as some of the world's most intensely rich and sweet wines – and everything in between. Both the Mosel and the Rhine Valley have numerous fabled vineyard sites. Elsewhere it is appreciated for its scent and citrus acidity, making excellent, generally dry wines in Australia, New Zealand, South Africa, New York State, Canada and France. Austria makes both sweet and dry versions.

SAUVIGNON BLANC

New Zealand has made this variety world-famous with its wonderfully tangy, crunchy dry whites, but Sauvignon originates in Bordeaux and the Loire Valley in France. It is now grown in cool conditions all over the world, usually in an attempt to ape the New Zealand style, which only burst on to the world stage in the 1980s, but sometimes as an oak-aged wine more in the style of a top Bordeaux white. Spain and Italy both grow it, but it prefers cooler conditions such as those of Austria and the Czech Republic. California and Australia are mostly a bit warm, but South Africa and Chile have found cool spots where it produces mouthwatering wines.

SÉMILLON

An important white grape in Bordeaux, both for dry whites and sweet Sauternes. It is normally blended with Sauvignon Blanc. The only other place to make a big success of it is Australia, especially in the Hunter Valley, where it makes a remarkable lemon zest, custard and toast crust-flavoured wine that demands aging.

VIOGNIER

Once hailed as the new Chardonnay, Viognier is no such thing. The wine is completely different – scented, with apricot and ripe pear fruit – and, unlike Chardonnay, it is very tricky to grow. There used to be just a few dozen hectares in the world, centred on Condrieu in France's northern Rhône, but it has now spread, having most success in Virginia, California, Argentina, South Africa and Australia. It is sometimes used to co-ferment with Syrah/Shiraz reds as is done traditionally in its homeland of Côte-Rôtie in the northern Rhône.

COMPOSITION OF A GRAPE

When it comes to imparting flavour to its wine, the actual juice of the grape rarely has very much to offer. Muscat juice is sweet and perfumed – that's why we eat Muscat grapes as well as make wine from them – but most of the great wine grapes of the world are no fun at all to eat. At best, a ripe wine grape has a sugary, neutral-flavoured, colourless pulp. Much of the character of a wine comes from its skin. As the grape ripens, the skin matures: its tannins become less aggressive, its colour deepens and all the perfume and flavour components build up. The trick is to try to ripen the grape so that sugar, acid, tannin, colour and flavour are all in balance at the time it is harvested. Both the pips and the stalks are very bitter, which is why modern winemakers usually de-stalk the grapes and avoid crushing the pips.

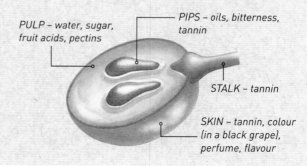

PULP – water, sugar, fruit acids, pectins

PIPS – oils, bitterness, tannin

STALK – tannin

SKIN – tannin, colour (in a black grape), perfume, flavour

WHITE WINES

The creation of any wine begins in the vineyard, but the winemaking process proper starts with the annual grape harvest. For white wines, this involves choices: pick early and make a snappily fresh wine for quick-drinking; or pursue ripeness until the grapes fill with sugar; or, in some parts of the world, leave the grapes to overripen and hope for an attack of the sweetness-intensifying noble rot.

In warmer wine regions, the sunshine that has ripened the grapes becomes the grapes' enemy as soon as they have been picked. White grapes are particularly vulnerable to oxidation. A common solution is to harvest at night or in the early morning when the air is at its coolest. You can then pile your grapes into a refrigerated truck if the winery is a long way away, and you can sprinkle antioxidants such as sulphur dioxide or ascorbic acid over the bunches to keep them in good condition. Some producers crush the grapes immediately and chill the resulting must at the vineyard.

CRUSHING AND PRESSING

Grapes destined for white wines generally need more careful handling than those for reds. The grapes should be crushed without too much force, and may then be left to steep for a while: juice, skin, pulp, pips and all, so that maximum grape flavour can be extracted from the skins where all the varietal flavour and character lie. This 'skin contact' may be as brief as an hour or as long as a day for white wine, and will vary between grape varieties, and also according to what is likely to happen to the wine afterwards: whether it will go into a new oak barrel or a steel tank, for instance.

Generally contact between juice and skins isn't required, so pressing forms part of the same process as crushing. The best quality juice emerges from the first, very gentle pressing. Further pressing will extract harsher elements from the skin as well as more juice – a bottled wine may be a blend of wines from different stages of pressing, according to the winemaker's requirements.

FERMENTATION

Once the juice has settled its solids, or been filtered or centrifuged to quicken the process (although filtration will invariably remove some potential flavour as well), it is pumped into a tank – generally of stainless steel, if the objective is to make a young fresh white. A suitable yeast culture is normally added to ensure the fermentation is both efficient and controlled and, in certain cases, to create particular nuances of flavour. Alternatively, wild yeasts may be allowed to work.

Stainless steel tanks are the easiest to keep sterile-clean, and in which to control temperature. The majority of white wines are fermented at cool temperatures to give a fruitier, fresher style, around 15–18°C (60–64°F), with the temperature kept down by running cold water or a coolant through insulated jackets or through coils within the tanks. Top Rieslings and Sauvignons rarely see oak, but in general, for the finest white wines, the juice is fermented at up to 25°C (77°F) in an oak barrel, which imparts a rich, mellow flavour even to a dry wine.

MALOLACTIC FERMENTATION

After the primary (alcoholic) fermentation, there is a second fermentation, the malolactic, in which green, appley, malic acid is turned into soft, creamy, lactic acid. Most classic whites undergo the malolactic, but as it reduces fresh-fruit character and tangy acidity it is often prevented in modern, fruit-driven whites, such as Rieslings and Sauvignons, by the use of filtration, low temperature or sulphur dioxide.

MATURING

Use of new oak *barriques* (225-litre barrels) is common, not just for aging the best wines of Burgundy or Bordeaux, but also for the sturdier styles of white wine, particularly Chardonnay, from all over the world. The great Sauvignon-Sémillon dry whites of Pessac-Léognan, as well as the luscious sweet wines of Sauternes, are also generally fermented and aged in oak. New oak gives a toasty, vanilla taste to wine and these days most bottles of good New World Chardonnay will have seen some oak during their fermentation and/or maturation. A final blend may consist of batches of wine which have spent time in new, one-year-old and two-year-old oak barrels, as well as some which have stayed in stainless steel. If the barrels are new, or fairly new, they give a strong, creamy or spicy character to the wine. Older barrels merely soften and round out the wine due to the slight contact with oxygen. This maturation can take up to 18 months but, in general, six months is quite long enough for a white wine.

BOTTLING

A wine for drinking young is generally stored in a stainless steel tank, racked off its lees if necessary, fined, filtered and then bottled – often at only six months old or less – to maximize its fresh, fruity character. Ideally, the very best wines are hardly filtered at all.

MUSCAT BLANC À PETITS GRAINS

The aristocrat of the Muscat family, this low yielder makes intensely grapy wines of more delicacy and fragrance than any of its cousins. It comes in all colours from white to brownish red, and can make delicate scented whites right through to rich, exotic, fortified wines the colour of burnt toffee. It is grown right throughout the Mediterranean, generally making scented sweet wines, but it also makes fizzy Asti in Italy and dry whites in Alto Adige and France's Alsace. It also makes some great fortified wines in Australia.

PINOT GRIS

Famous – or notorious – nowadays as Pinot Grigio, a light, mild, thirst-quencher from northern Italy and Eastern Europe. However, as Pinot Gris in France's Alsace, it makes serious, honeyed golden wines of considerable power. New Zealand also makes some weighty Pinot Gris, but mostly the lighter style is followed, in Romania, Slovenia, Hungary, England and Germany as well as in British Columbia, Oregon, Washington State and (usually as Pinot Grigio) in California and Australia.

RIESLING

Cold-resistant, late-ripening grape that makes thrilling, delicate wines in Germany as fleeting as gossamer and as low as 7.5 per cent in alcohol, as well as some of the world's most intensely rich and sweet wines – and everything in between. Both the Mosel and the Rhine Valley have numerous fabled vineyard sites. Elsewhere it is appreciated for its scent and citrus acidity, making excellent, generally dry wines in Australia, New Zealand, South Africa, New York State, Canada and France. Austria makes both sweet and dry versions.

SAUVIGNON BLANC

New Zealand has made this variety world-famous with its wonderfully tangy, crunchy dry whites, but Sauvignon originates in Bordeaux and the Loire Valley in France. It is now grown in cool conditions all over the world, usually in an attempt to ape the New Zealand style, which only burst on to the world stage in the 1980s, but sometimes as an oak-aged wine more in the style of a top Bordeaux white. Spain and Italy both grow it, but it prefers cooler conditions such as those of Austria and the Czech Republic. California and Australia are mostly a bit warm, but South Africa and Chile have found cool spots where it produces mouthwatering wines.

SÉMILLON

An important white grape in Bordeaux, both for dry whites and sweet Sauternes. It is normally blended with Sauvignon Blanc. The only other place to make a big success of it is Australia, especially in the Hunter Valley, where it makes a remarkable lemon zest, custard and toast crust-flavoured wine that demands aging.

VIOGNIER

Once hailed as the new Chardonnay, Viognier is no such thing. The wine is completely different – scented, with apricot and ripe pear fruit – and, unlike Chardonnay, it is very tricky to grow. There used to be just a few dozen hectares in the world, centred on Condrieu in France's northern Rhône, but it has now spread, having most success in Virginia, California, Argentina, South Africa and Australia. It is sometimes used to co-ferment with Syrah/Shiraz reds as is done traditionally in its homeland of Côte-Rôtie in the northern Rhône.

COMPOSITION OF A GRAPE

When it comes to imparting flavour to its wine, the actual juice of the grape rarely has very much to offer. Muscat juice is sweet and perfumed – that's why we eat Muscat grapes as well as make wine from them – but most of the great wine grapes of the world are no fun at all to eat. At best, a ripe wine grape has a sugary, neutral-flavoured, colourless pulp. Much of the character of a wine comes from its skin. As the grape ripens, the skin matures: its tannins become less aggressive, its colour deepens and all the perfume and flavour components build up. The trick is to try to ripen the grape so that sugar, acid, tannin, colour and flavour are all in balance at the time it is harvested. Both the pips and the stalks are very bitter, which is why modern winemakers usually de-stalk the grapes and avoid crushing the pips.

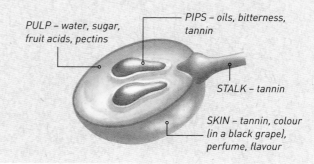

PULP – water, sugar, fruit acids, pectins

PIPS – oils, bitterness, tannin

STALK – tannin

SKIN – tannin, colour (in a black grape), perfume, flavour

In the Vineyard

ANYONE PLANTING GRAPES to make wine must ask two questions. What will the natural conditions (geography, geology, soil, climate) of my vineyard allow me to achieve? What do I, as a winemaker, want to achieve? Winemakers in the world's classic vineyard areas have developed their wine styles over the centuries by endlessly asking and answering these questions. Today the world of wine is turbulent with change; yet these two questions are as important as ever.

A grape variety is chosen primarily for its ripening qualities: its ability to ripen at all in cooler areas, like Germany, or its ability to resist overripening in hot areas, like the Mediterranean. The interaction of grape variety and climate produces a staggering spectrum of results. The Greeks might pick Liatiko grapes in July while the

Deep beds of gravel are warm and provide good drainage, which is vital in Bordeaux's damp maritime climate and can make all the difference between good and mediocre wine.

Germans fill in time between Christmas and New Year bringing in their late, late Riesling for Eiswein.

Given that, genetically, the 5,000 or so grape varieties identified so far as remotely connected with wine production are all different and react differently to soil and climate, let's look at these two basics and how they affect the siting of the vineyards.

SOIL

Many traditional producers consider soil the most important factor in the creation of great wine. Christian Moueix, who makes some of the world's most exclusive red wines in Pomerol in Bordeaux, reckons soil contributes 80 per cent of the quality; others dismiss this view, particularly in places such as California, Australia and New Zealand, where the link between soil and personality is not as yet proven by generations of experience. The truth is generally somewhere in between. There is no doubt that in certain remarkable vineyards the soil is unique and capable of shaping a wine's flavour. However, these 'chemical' and 'mineral' component parts defy analysis: in the Burgundy Grands Crus great efforts have been made to explain variations in flavour from vines in different parts of the same vineyard – with no success.

On the other hand, the physical attributes of soil are more easily defined and are, in general, more significant. Most important of these is drainage. Well-drained soil – slate or gravel or chalk – pushes the vine roots down and down to find moisture. Furthermore, porous soils are generally poor – another reason for roots thrusting deep, this time in search of nourishment. The result is a stable environment way below the surface, which makes the vine itself less vulnerable to stress from drought and flood. Riesling likes slate, Cabernet likes gravel, Chardonnay likes limestone or chalk – all of them drain well.

A dry soil is also a warmer soil. This is crucial in cool-climate regions where the stones which break up the soil and boost porosity also retain vital heat. Gravel in the Médoc and slate on the Mosel aid drainage and store heat for the chilly autumn evenings. In Bordeaux the late-ripening Cabernet Sauvignon – which thrives on the Médoc gravel – cannot ripen on the heavy cold clay of St-Émilion and Pomerol, where the quick-ripening Merlot rules supreme. However, for this reason, clay's coolness is useful in hot areas: Chardonnay, which grows well in

Burgundy only on limestone, can grow very well on clay in hotter areas. Light-coloured soils, such as chalk and limestone, will reflect back heat.

CLIMATE

The second major influence is climate: water and warmth. Since wine, at its most basic, is rain-water sucked up and transformed by the vine (picking up a bit of flavour from the soil on the way), too little water means not enough juice. Either you irrigate – a common practice in America and the southern hemisphere (but largely forbidden in Europe except for 'experimental' purposes) – or you choose a favourable site, somewhere with a reliable rainfall, a porous top soil, and water-retentive subsoil underneath. Since such geological balance is rare and the weather generally unreliable, this perfect combination is seldom achieved. Too much water, however, is far worse than too little, because all you can do then is watch as your grapes swell and swell with excessive liquid. Just before vintage time, especially, rainstorms, which dilute the character of the juice by swelling the grapes, can have a seriously bad effect on wine quality.

Obviously heat is essential to ripen grapes. But different varieties need different amounts, and though lack of sun is the chief problem in the traditional 'classic' regions of Europe, in most other areas, such as Australia and South America, a surfeit of sun can make the grapes ripen too fast, before they have picked up enough character and flavour from the soil, and before a good balance of grape sugar and acidity has been achieved.

SITING THE VINEYARD

In cool areas, you want to maximize warmth. Consequently rows are ideally planted on a north-south axis to catch the midday sun. The best slopes may incline south-eastwards, as in Burgundy, for the morning sun to warm the vineyards; or south-westwards as in Germany's Rheingau, where morning mists shroud the vines and so late afternoon sun becomes all important. To conserve heat the vines are planted close together and trained low; they are also aligned across the prevailing wind, so that precious warmth doesn't get blown out of the rows. Hot climates demand the opposite. Vineyards frequently face away from the sun and are trained high with lots of foliage to shade the grapes; they are also spaced further apart so that heat can disperse and what little water there is will not be divided among too many plants. The norm in 'new' areas is about 1,000 vines to the hectare; in Burgundy it is 10,000 to the hectare! Somewhere between 3,000 and 5,000 is probably about right in most places.

ALTERNATIVE TECHNIQUES

Biodynamism: Biodynamic vineyards are loony fringe or at the heart of the ecological movement, depending on your viewpoint, but many of the world's finest winemakers have adopted their methods. These involve applying biodynamic preparations to the vines and carrying out specific tasks according to a biodynamic calendar influenced by earthly, solar and celestial movements. Many of the wines are outstanding.

Organic: Organic methods primarily apply to the vineyard rather than the winery, and different countries have different regulations. 'Organic wine' in the USA and Canada, for instance, cannot include sulphur, though it can in Europe. The crux of the movement is the decision not to use non-organic fertilizers, herbicides, fungicides or pesticides. The objective is a chemical-free vineyard and one without any GM material. Many vineyards operate on relatively organic lines, particularly in the fairly disease-free New World.

Natural wine: The biggest objection I have to the 'natural wine' movement is the self-righteous way many supporters declaim that any wine not made their way is unnaturally and potentially toxic. This is nonsense. The world of wine is a broad church, in which 'natural wine' is a welcome member. The objectives of natural wine are entirely laudable – a desire to return to the pre-industrial, pre-technological and chemical world. A little use of sulphur is sometimes tolerated. The result is some strikingly pure wines, some fascinatingly rustic wines and some wines too dominated by wine faults to be attractive to anyone but the most obsessive devotee.

Orange wine: White wine is usually made from juice quickly pressed off the skins before fermentation. Orange wines are white wines made more like red, with the juice fermenting and aging together with the pips, skins and maybe stalks. The result is wines of most unusual personality, chewy and bitter from the tannin in the pips, skins and stalks, and with flavours more to do with sap and earth and dried out fruits and herbs than the typical fresh modern whites. The colour can be orange, but doesn't have to be. Wines from Georgia produced like this in earthenware 'Queri' pots have made such wines fashionable, and orange wines have been made in Friuli in north-east Italy since 1998. Many countries are now having a go, often with excellent results. But they're not like your average House White.

A YEAR IN THE VINEYARD

Whether or not your vineyard – planted with the right grapes in the right place – actually produces great wine depends on your year-long efforts and your luck with the endless vagaries of the weather. So let's look at a typical vineyard year in a temperate European area like Bordeaux. The year starts straight after the grape harvest, in November: that's what growers call the beginning of winter.

WINTER

After the exhilaration and hyperactivity of the vintage, there's a hiatus. Winemaking becomes the priority. The vines relax, exhausted, as the temperature drops. At below 11°C (52°F), the vine gradually becomes dormant and will be quite safe in this state down to a minimum of –28°C (–18°F). Now is the time for lopping off the long branches – they make ideal fuel for grilling meat and fish next spring; for manuring; for ploughing, especially in cold areas where earth is heaped up around the base of the vine for protection against frost; and, on steep slopes, for redistributing soil washed down by heavy rains. In some vineyards December sees the start of pruning. If you prune severely you will get far less fruit, but far

higher quality. Old or weak vines may require more lenient treatment, but the experienced pruner – with next year's vintage in mind – will assess each vine's capacity and cut accordingly.

January comes. The bone-chilling job of pruning back the vines continues. As February shuffles in, thoughts of springtime and the world alive again begin to get the better of the fierce damp winds.

The last job of winter is to take cuttings for grafting on to rootstocks. In Europe especially, grafting is the only effective way of protecting *Vitis vinifera* – the vine species used for all serious winemaking. You have to do this because of a vine aphid, *Phylloxera vastatrix* (wonderful name) which came from America in the 1860s and proceeded to eat its way through all of Europe's vineyards, and most of the rest of the world's as well. The sole remedy was – and still is – to graft European *vinifera* cuttings on to rootstocks of American varieties which, since phylloxera has transatlantic origins, can tolerate the nasty little beast. Without this grafting system, there would be no fine wine made in Europe today!

SPRING

March is when the vine wakes up: sap rises and the pruned shoots drip with 'tears'. Pruning can be finished without

Harvesting Cabernet Sauvignon in the Colchagua Valley, one of Chile's warmest regions and well suited to Cabernet.

coat and scarf, and the soil can at last be worked again to give it a good airing and to uncover the base of the vines. Frosts in March aren't too much of a threat, but in April – when buds burst and shoots begin to emerge – they're far more menacing. You'll also have to start spraying against insects and disease, because the vine isn't the only thing to wake up with the spring: its predators are on the move again – spiders, bugs and beetles are out looking for food.

May brings hopes and fears in equal proportion. The shoots lengthen by the hour, leaves and tendrils sprout, and the first signs of the flower buds appear. Yet you must temper optimism with prudence. In a typical non-organic vineyard you must begin to spray against the two fungi, downy and powdery mildew (*peronospera* and *oidium*). From now on you'll be spraying against one threat or another right through to autumn. The weeds will be enjoying the spring sunshine and you'll have to deal with those, too.

And you'll be on the phone to the local weather office. Is there a risk of frost? The vine shoots can be killed outright by a late May frost and the harvest will be devastated. In areas like Chablis in Burgundy, the Rhine in Germany, and the Napa Valley in California, they use stoves, flame guns, torches and great propellers to stop the frozen air sliding into the hollows and murdering the young vines. In some places they continually spray the vines with water, which freezes into ice around the buds and so keeps the temperature at zero. Uncomfortable for us, but just about OK for a young vine.

SUMMER

Then it's summer. You want sun right through June because this is when the vine flowers. If it pours during this crucial 10–14 day period, the flowers will not be fertilized: the bunches of grapes – and consequently the vintage – will be drastically reduced. Once flowering is over you thin the shoots, keeping only the best, and tie them to wires to shape their growth. Throughout the long 100-day haul from flowering to within striking distance of the harvest, spraying continues.

In July, you till the land again, and also trim back excessive growth and vegetation so that you don't get too many grapes, which will dilute quality – unless you don't care, in which case you go on holiday.

Some vignerons never seem to go on holiday at all, but August is the most usual month to take time off. However, someone should be there, spraying and thinning the bunches. The grapes are changing colour, softening and gaining sugar. Yet hail can sweep up and ravage your vines without warning, while wet, warm weather can cause the onset of rot.

Sorting Pinot Noir at Helan Mountain, one of several boutique wineries in China making huge improvements in quality in recent years.

AUTUMN

Vintage looms! It may be September, it may be October. In the winery everyone is feverishly preparing equipment. Outdoors the temptation is to sit in the sun, chew the grapes and dream of great things. But you must keep at it. Greatness is within your grasp: make a last spray against rot, check daily for insect invasion, and keep the birds off – by nets, by scarecrows, by shotguns – but keep them off! It's your livelihood they're eating.

Then at last – the great day. Vintage starts. Out go the tractors, the troops of pickers, or maybe the giant harvesting machine, to pluck the results of another year's labour. Hand-pickers cut the bunches off, then place them in boxes or baskets for collection. Depending on the height of the vines, the work is either back-breaking or knee-creasing and, depending on the time of day, cripplingly cold in the morning mist but happily hot in the afternoon sun. Mechanical harvesters, straddling the rows, knock the grapes off with fibreglass rods. And as the grapes arrive at the winery, good will be separated from bad on the sorting tables or by optical lasers.

Whatever the method, as the grapes pile up you are looking at your due reward or just desserts – nature's bounty or nature's revenge.

In the Winery

RED AND ROSÉ WINES

Wine is created by fermentation – yeasts turning grape sugar into alcohol. If you bought a few bunches of ripe grapes, squashed them, put the resulting goo into a bucket and left it somewhere warm like the airing cupboard – well, a wine of sorts would almost certainly be produced. It might taste more like vinegar, but technically it would be wine. This simple chemical reaction has been refined by hundreds of years of experience and, more recently, by high technology and microbiological know-how. It is difficult to generalize about winemaking styles and methods in countries and states as diverse as New Zealand and Texas, Argentina and Tasmania. What France or Italy may regard as old hat, the wineries of Brazil or Mexico may barely have begun to think about. At every stage, even the most technocratic winemaker indulges in little personal adjustments – in all but the drabbest corporate winemaker lurks an artist's soul – each of which affect the final character of the wine. But some techniques are standard around the globe.

CRUSHING

The winemaking process begins when the grapes arrive. With the exception of Beaujolais and a few other wines using the 'whole bunch' method of fermentation (also called carbonic maceration), red grapes are put through a crusher to break their skins and release the juice. The crushing machine usually also removes the stalks, as these are bitter, but they can also have a delightful sappy flavour, and with some grapes, notably Syrah and Pinot Noir, a proportion is sometimes left on. The resulting 'must' – pulpy mush of flesh and juice and skins (which give red and rosé wines their colour) – is pumped into a big vat, ready for fermentation.

FERMENTATION

Fermentation is caused by the action of yeasts on the sugars in the grape juice. Yeasts are naturally present in the vineyards and winery, but, cultivated yeasts are generally used to ensure a controlled fermentation. At this stage, in the cooler areas of Europe, the addition of sugar is permitted if the sugar content of the grapes is too low, to increase alcoholic strength, a process called chaptalization. Similarly, in very hot regions, a little acid may be added if the grapes are very ripe.

For rosé wines, the fermenting juice is drawn off the skins after a day or so and the winemaking process then follows the same path as for white wines (see page 24).

Fermentation lasts from a few days to a few weeks, depending on the yeast culture and cellar temperature. Temperature control is one of the most crucial tools available to the modern winemaker, and the introduction of stainless steel tanks and refrigeration in the 1950s were major breakthroughs in winemaking. Heat is needed to extract colour from the skins, but excess heat destroys freshness and fruit flavour, and can disrupt the fermentation process itself. Should the winemaker choose a cultured or a wild yeast? Modern cultured yeasts are controllable and produce specific results. Beneficial wild yeast strains have developed over centuries and quality producers are increasingly favouring these.

Throughout the process, the grape skins surge upwards, pushed by the stream of carbon dioxide released during fermentation. At the top, they form a thick 'cap' which must be mixed back in continually by punching down or pumping the juice over the cap, so that the wine can extract maximum colour and flavour and avoid air becoming trapped between the skins and the wine. Many red wines, including all those intended for long aging, are left to macerate on the skins for some days or weeks after fermentation is complete, in order to extract all the flavour, colour and tannin from the skins and pips; long maceration also softens the harsh tannins.

PRESSING

When red wine fermentation is finished – all the sugar having been converted to alcohol – the wine is drawn off the vat, and the residue of skins is pressed, to produce a dark, tannic wine called 'press wine'. This may be used for blending and added to the free-run wine to create a deeper, tougher style of wine, or it may be stored apart.

MALOLACTIC FERMENTATION

Technically, the wine is now made – but it is pretty raw stuff. To begin with, it probably has a sharp, green-apple acidity. This is reduced through the 'malolactic' fermentation which converts that tart malic acid into

Almost everywhere in the world where white wine is made the juice is fermented in large, refrigerated stainless steel tanks. These ones are at Château Haut-Brion in Bordeaux.

variety, but blend grapes from different vineyards. This may be done in order to achieve a consistent style, or to balance the varying characteristics of the grapes.

The decision on whether to mature a wine in stainless steel or oak is of enormous stylistic importance. Stainless steel (or concrete) is inert and amenable to accurate temperature control, which allows the fruit flavours free rein. Small oak barrels allow controlled oxygenation and benign aging of what might otherwise be unduly aggressive wines, as well as adding flavours of vanilla and toast.

If the wine is to be drunk young, it is put in large tanks of stainless steel or concrete to rest a short while before bottling. Almost all rosé is treated in this way. Red wine for aging, however, is stored – often in small oak barrels (*barriques*) – for anything from a few months to over two years. If the *barriques* are new or only once-used, they impart flavours of spice, herbs, perfume and vanilla as well as adding to the wine's tannic structure.

RACKING, FINING AND FILTERING

During this pre-bottling period, dead yeast cells and other solids fall to the bottom of the tank or barrel. These are separated from the wine by racking – transferring the wine to clean barrels or tanks – which may take place several times before bottling. Racking naturally mixes oxygen with the wine and this usually clears out any sulphuric or yeasty flavours.

With many top-quality wines, the last stage before bottling is 'fining': removing any particles held in suspension by means of a clarifying agent. The agent – typically egg white or bentonite – is spread over the surface and, as it falls down through the wine, it collects all impurities with it. Most other wines are also filtered; those for immediate drinking often receive quite a fierce filtration to ensure no deposit forms in the bottle. Some of the best wines are filtered, but very lightly. Some top red wines are neither fined nor filtered and so develop a harmless deposit in the bottle. Wines with residual sweetness will be tightly sterile filtered.

BOTTLING

For best results, bottling should be cold and sterile, with an inert gas like nitrogen or carbon dioxide, introduced into the bottle ahead of the wine so that when the cork goes in there is no oxygen in the bottle. Some of the cheapest wines are either 'hot-bottled' or pasteurized. Both treatments ensure the wine's stability but detract from its personality and make any further development impossible. Cork or screwcap may be the preferred closure.

mild lactic acid. Almost all reds undergo this second fermentation, becoming softer and rounder. It occurs naturally when temperatures rise in the spring following the harvest, but is often induced soon after the alcoholic fermentation, by raising the temperature in the cellar and by adding the appropriate bacteria.

BLENDING AND MATURING

The winemaker can alter the wine radically by blending the contents of two or more vats together. That could mean combining different grape varieties to add a whole new dimension of flavour. Some wines use only one

WHITE WINES

The creation of any wine begins in the vineyard, but the winemaking process proper starts with the annual grape harvest. For white wines, this involves choices: pick early and make a snappily fresh wine for quick-drinking; or pursue ripeness until the grapes fill with sugar; or, in some parts of the world, leave the grapes to overripen and hope for an attack of the sweetness-intensifying noble rot.

In warmer wine regions, the sunshine that has ripened the grapes becomes the grapes' enemy as soon as they have been picked. White grapes are particularly vulnerable to oxidation. A common solution is to harvest at night or in the early morning when the air is at its coolest. You can then pile your grapes into a refrigerated truck if the winery is a long way away, and you can sprinkle antioxidants such as sulphur dioxide or ascorbic acid over the bunches to keep them in good condition. Some producers crush the grapes immediately and chill the resulting must at the vineyard.

CRUSHING AND PRESSING

Grapes destined for white wines generally need more careful handling than those for reds. The grapes should be crushed without too much force, and may then be left to steep for a while: juice, skin, pulp, pips and all, so that maximum grape flavour can be extracted from the skins where all the varietal flavour and character lie. This 'skin contact' may be as brief as an hour or as long as a day for white wine, and will vary between grape varieties, and also according to what is likely to happen to the wine afterwards: whether it will go into a new oak barrel or a steel tank, for instance.

Generally contact between juice and skins isn't required, so pressing forms part of the same process as crushing. The best quality juice emerges from the first, very gentle pressing. Further pressing will extract harsher elements from the skin as well as more juice – a bottled wine may be a blend of wines from different stages of pressing, according to the winemaker's requirements.

FERMENTATION

Once the juice has settled its solids, or been filtered or centrifuged to quicken the process (although filtration will invariably remove some potential flavour as well), it is pumped into a tank – generally of stainless steel, if the objective is to make a young fresh white. A suitable yeast culture is normally added to ensure the fermentation is both efficient and controlled and, in certain cases, to create particular nuances of flavour. Alternatively, wild yeasts may be allowed to work.

Stainless steel tanks are the easiest to keep sterile-clean, and in which to control temperature. The majority of white wines are fermented at cool temperatures to give a fruitier, fresher style, around 15–18°C (60–64°F), with the temperature kept down by running cold water or a coolant through insulated jackets or through coils within the tanks. Top Rieslings and Sauvignons rarely see oak, but in general, for the finest white wines, the juice is fermented at up to 25°C (77°F) in an oak barrel, which imparts a rich, mellow flavour even to a dry wine.

MALOLACTIC FERMENTATION

After the primary (alcoholic) fermentation, there is a second fermentation, the malolactic, in which green, appley, malic acid is turned into soft, creamy, lactic acid. Most classic whites undergo the malolactic, but as it reduces fresh-fruit character and tangy acidity it is often prevented in modern, fruit-driven whites, such as Rieslings and Sauvignons, by the use of filtration, low temperature or sulphur dioxide.

MATURING

Use of new oak *barriques* (225-litre barrels) is common, not just for aging the best wines of Burgundy or Bordeaux, but also for the sturdier styles of white wine, particularly Chardonnay, from all over the world. The great Sauvignon-Sémillon dry whites of Pessac-Léognan, as well as the luscious sweet wines of Sauternes, are also generally fermented and aged in oak. New oak gives a toasty, vanilla taste to wine and these days most bottles of good New World Chardonnay will have seen some oak during their fermentation and/or maturation. A final blend may consist of batches of wine which have spent time in new, one-year-old and two-year-old oak barrels, as well as some which have stayed in stainless steel. If the barrels are new, or fairly new, they give a strong, creamy or spicy character to the wine. Older barrels merely soften and round out the wine due to the slight contact with oxygen. This maturation can take up to 18 months but, in general, six months is quite long enough for a white wine.

BOTTLING

A wine for drinking young is generally stored in a stainless steel tank, racked off its lees if necessary, fined, filtered and then bottled – often at only six months old or less – to maximize its fresh, fruity character. Ideally, the very best wines are hardly filtered at all.

SWEET WINES

The great sweet wines of France, Germany, Austria and occasionally Australia, New Zealand and the USA, are made from grapes that are left on the vine well after the normal harvest, so they are overripe and full of sugar; they also begin to shrivel, which concentrates the sugar. The best are attacked by a fungus called 'noble rot' (*Botrytis cinerea*). This sucks out the water, concentrating the sugar even more. During fermentation, the sugar is converted by yeasts into alcohol: the more sugar in the grape juice, the higher the potential alcoholic strength. But yeasts can only work in alcohol levels of up to about 15 per cent. So when the yeasts stop, the rest of the grape sugar remains in the wine as sweetness – full of potential lusciousness.

Hungary's intensely sweet Tokaji is also made using botrytized grapes, which are added to a dry base wine. Another method of making wine sweet is traditional in parts of Italy (where it is known as *passito* or *recioto*) and in the Jura, France (for *vin de paille*). After picking, the grapes are laid on mats or in shallow trays, or the bunches are hung from rafters. They begin to dry out, losing water, which concentrates all the other constituents, especially the sugars.

Remuage, *an important process in the Champagne method.*

FORTIFIED WINES

Fortified wines have a neutral alcohol spirit added to them after partial or full fermentation to raise their alcohol level to between 16 and 24 per cent. Yeasts cannot operate at more than about 15–16 per cent alcohol, so fermentation stops and any remaining sugar stays in the wine as sweetness. Sherry can be sweet or dry, but most of the finest ones are dry, and the fortification is done when the fermentation is finished, serving to stablize the wine for what can be a lengthy maturing process.

Port is usually sweet. The high strength spirit is added before the fermentation has finished, raising the alcohol level to about 19 per cent, and leaving a lot of sugar sweetness still in the wine. Wines are aged primarily in barrel or in bottle depending on their style. Madeira can be sweet or dry. It gains its smoky, almost burnt flavour through an aging process that includes warming the wine to imitate its traditional passage across the Equator on sailing ships. France makes sweet fortified wines along the Mediterranean coast and in the Rhône Valley and Australia makes mighty versions in north-east Victoria.

SPARKLING WINES

Carbon dioxide is given off during fermentation and if the fermenting wine is kept in a pressurized container the gas is absorbed by the wine – for as long as the pressure remains. That explains why as soon as you open a bottle of sparkling wine there is a whoosh of bubbles as the pressure is released. All the greatest sparklers are made by inducing a second fermentation in the final bottle. This is called the Champagne, traditional or classic method. The still wine is bottled with a little sugar and yeast to restart the fermentation, tightly sealed (often with a crown cap) and stored in a cool cellar from a few months to several years. The second fermentation occurs and the carbon dioxide bubbles dissolve in the wine, but the yeast cells die and are deposited as sludge on the inside of the bottle. So the bottle undergoes 'remuage' – being twisted, tapped and turned on their heads to move all the sludge to the bottle neck. The sludge is then disgorged – the neck of the bottle is frozen in brine, the stopper is removed and the pellet of sludge pops out. The bottle is topped up – you can add a 'dosage' of wine and sugar to adjust the sweetness – and put a proper cork in, wire it down and you're done.

Cheaper fizz, such as Asti or Prosecco, is made by creating the second fermentation in a large tank – the 'tank' or Charmat method.

What does it taste like?

WHEN YOU BUY WINE, buy it for its flavour. Reputation, packaging and price all vie to influence your choice, but they can't titillate your tastebuds. The grape variety used is the most significant factor in determining the taste of a wine, but everything that happens to the grapes and their juice on the long journey from the vine to the glass in your hand contributes to that wine's unique identity. Read on and start getting the flavour you want.

GET THE FLAVOUR YOU WANT

Your chances of walking into a wine shop and coming out with a wine that's enjoyable to drink, whatever the price level, are better now than ever before. The last quarter of the 20th century saw a revolution in wine, in terms of both style and quality from which we are all now benefitting. All wines are cleaner and fresher-tasting than they were; reds are juicier, rounder and softer; whites are snappier, zestier, more appetizing. There are more new oak barrels being used in expensive wines, which in terms of taste means nutty vanilla and buttered toast. But all wines don't taste alike. Indeed, there's never been a wider choice. It's just that modern winemaking is rapidly eliminating faults – it's not eliminating individuality.

So how do you choose? How do you tell a wine that's just right for summer lunch in the garden from one that would be better suited to a winter evening in front of a log fire? Well, imagine if you could walk into a wine shop and just pick up a bottle from the 'green, tangy white' shelf or go for a 'spicy, warm-hearted red'. That would make things pretty easy, wouldn't it?

You see, all those thousands of different flavours fall into the 18 broad styles shown here. So, even if you don't yet know much about grape varieties and wine-producing regions, just choose a style that appeals and I'll try to point you in the right direction.

RED WINES

1 JUICY, FRUITY REDS

Refreshing, approachable and delicious – tasty, refreshing reds are ideal for gulping down with or without food, emphasizing bright fruit flavours and minimizing the gum-drying toughness of tannin.

This style had its birth in the New World but it has spread right through Europe, overturning any lingering ideas that red wine must be aged. You don't age these wines. You buy them and you drink them. Chilean Merlot is the benchmark: young, well-balanced, and bursting with blackberry, blackcurrant and plum flavours. Spain produces lots of inexpensive soft, supple reds in the same mould, from La Mancha, Jumilla, Campo de Borja or Calatayud. Try young Valpolicella and Teroldego from Italy and unoaked reds from Portugal's Douro region. California does young Merlots and Zinfandels and Argentina has smooth Tempranillo, ultra-fruity Bonarda and juicy Malbec. Beaujolais is famous for this style in France. Loire Valley reds have sharper, but very refreshing fruit and Languedoc Merlot can be good.

2 SILKY, STRAWBERRYISH REDS

Mellow, perfumed reds with a gentle strawberry, raspberry or cherry fruit fragrance and flavour. Good ones feel silky in your mouth.

Pinot Noir is the grape that produces the supreme examples of this style. Its home territory is Burgundy in France (Bourgogne in French). Virtually all red Burgundy is made from Pinot Noir. Beyond Burgundy the best Pinot Noir comes from California – particularly Carneros, Sonoma Coast, Russian River and Santa Barbara – and from Oregon, Chile, New Zealand and, occasionally, Australia. Germany can nowadays hit the spot, too, and England is beginning to work it out. Cheap Pinot Noir is rarely good, but Chile's usually have loads of vibrant jellied fruit flavour. Red Rioja and Navarra, from Spain but made from different grapes, principally Tempranillo, can be soft and smooth with a fragrant strawberryish quality. This also appears in the lightest Côtes du Rhône-Villages from France.

3 INTENSE, BLACKCURRANTY REDS

Full-flavoured red wines with a distinctive blackcurrant flavour and those slightly bitter tannins from the grape skins that dry your mouth but make it water at the same time. They're made from Cabernet Sauvignon alone or blended with Merlot and other grapes to enrich the fruit flavours and soften the texture.

The Cabernet-based red wines of Bordeaux in France are the original blackcurranty wines with, at their best, a fragrance of cigar boxes and lead pencils. New World Cabernets have more blackcurrant, but also a vanilla-y flavour and sometimes mint. Cabernet Sauvignon is one of the most reliable wines you can get. It retains its characteristic flavours wherever it's from, and at every price level – and that's rare in wine. Expensive ones should be ripe and rich with layers of intense flavour; cheaper ones have simpler flavours that are more earthy, more jammy, or more green-pepper lean. For budget Cabernets, check out Argentina, Chile, Australia, South Africa and France's Pays d'Oc. Bordeaux, Chile, Argentina, South Africa, New Zealand, Australia and California at the higher price level are outstanding. You'll also find these blackcurrant flavours in Spain's Ribera del Duero, from the Tempranillo grape, and a number of grapes, especially Touriga Nacional, give black fruit flavours in Portugal.

4 SPICY, WARM-HEARTED REDS

Dense, heartwarming, gloriously rich flavours of blackberry and loganberry, black pepper and chocolate, and mainly found in Syrah/Shiraz.

Australian Shiraz is the wine to try: often dense, rich and chocolaty, sometimes fresher, with peppery, blackberry fruit, sometimes with a whiff of smoke or a slap of leather. In France's Rhône Valley the same grape is called Syrah. Rhône Syrah tends to be a little more austere in style, and smoky-minerally to Australia's rich spice, but the best have lush blackberry fruit. Look for the label Crozes-Hermitage or St-Joseph. For good value from France try Pays d'Oc Syrah, Faugères or Minervois. Portugal offers good value with a whole host of indigenous grape varieties. In Spain, try the weighty plums and vanilla flavours of Toro and the more expensive Montsant and Priorat. California Zinfandel and Petite Sirah are powerful, spicy and rich. Argentina's heart-warming Malbecs and Chile's great big spicy-savoury mouthfuls of Carmenère are excellent value. Take a look at South Africa's smoky Pinotage, too.

5 MOUTHWATERING, HERBY REDS

Intriguing wines with a rasping herby bite and sweet-sour red fruit flavours – Italian reds do this better than any others.

There's a rasp of sourness in these reds that's intended to cut through steak or pasta sauce, not be sipped as an apéritif. You'll find that same irresistible sour-cherries edge on wines made from all sorts of grapes – Dolcetto, Sangiovese, Barbera, Teroldego, Lagrein and Refosco. Some may have a delicious raisiny taste, too. Even light, low tannin Valpolicella has this flavour. Up in Piedmont, tough, tannic wines from Barolo and Barbaresco, made from the stern Nebbiolo grape, have a fascinating tar-and-roses flavour. A decent Langhe will give you the flavour for less money. Down in the South, grapes like Negroamaro and Primitivo add round, pruny flavours to the sour-cherry bite. Sicilian reds, especially Nero d'Avola, are rich and mouthfilling.

6 EARTHY, SAVOURY REDS

These are the classic food wines of Europe, the kind where fruit flavours often take a back seat to compatibility with food and the ability to cleanse the palate and stimulate the appetite.

France, especially Bordeaux, is the leader in this style. Even at the top end most Bordeaux reds keep an earthy quality underpinning their richness. Even St-Émilion and

Pomerol generally blend attractive savouriness with lush fruit. Wines from Haut-Médoc, Médoc, Pessac-Léognan and Graves on Bordeaux's Left Bank have stony or earthy flavours. Côtes de Bourg, Blaye and basic Bordeaux and Bordeaux Supérieur are usually marked by earthy, savoury qualities. You can find these flavours all over South-West France, too.

Italy's main earthy, savoury type is Chianti. Basic Sangiovese, Montepulciano and Barbera wines throughout Italy often share this trait. Croatian, Romanian and Hungarian Merlot are refreshingly earthy, Greek reds almost stony, and the more basic reds of northern Portugal and Spain follow this line. In the New World fruit is riper and generally too rich for many of these styles, but some Cabernets and Merlots from places like Canada, New York, Washington State, New Zealand, South Africa and even China may fit the bill.

ROSÉ WINES

7 DELICATE ROSÉS

Good rosé should be fragrant and refreshing, and deliciously dry – not sickly and sweet.

France is a good hunting ground for this style of wine. Attractive, slightly leafy-tasting Bordeaux Rosé and Rosé de Loire are lovely dry wines. Elegant Pinot Noir rosés come from Sancerre in the eastern Loire and Marsannay at the northern end of the Côte de Nuits in Burgundy. The southern Rhône Valley produces plenty of dry but fruity rosés. Côtes de Provence is dry, beguilingly smooth but often expensive. Bandol and Bellet are pricier still – but tastier too. Northern Italy produces light, fresh pale rosé called chiaretto, from Bardolino high in the Dolomites from Lagrein. Garnacha rosado from Navarra and Rioja in northern Spain are tasty. And English pinks are coming on nicely.

8 GUTSY ROSÉS

Dry, fruity rosé can be wonderful, with flavours of strawberries and maybe raspberries and rosehips, cherries, apples and herbs, too. More colour, more fruit flavour, more texture to roll around your mouth. Spain, Chile, Australia and New Zealand do best.

Most countries make a dry rosé, and any red grape will do. Grenache/Garnacha or Tempranillo from Spain is often excellent. Puglia and Sicily in southern Italy make mouthfilling rosés, too. France has big, strong, dry rosés from Tavel and Lirac in the southern Rhône Valley. South

America is a good bet for flavoursome, fruit-forward pink wines as are fruity Australian Grenaches from the Barossa Valley, or New Zealand pinks.

9 SWEET ROSÉS

Blush is the usual name, and most of it comes from California as Zinfandel. Anjou Rosé is France's version.

Zinfandel from California, which is often described as 'blush', is fairly sweet. Other sweetish rosés are Rosé d'Anjou from the Loire Valley and Portuguese rosés such as Mateus and Lancers.

WHITE WINES

10 BONE-DRY, NEUTRAL WHITES

Crisp, refreshing whites whose flavours won't set the world alight – but chill them down and set them next to a plate of shellfish and you've got the perfect combination.

In France, Muscadet from the Loire Valley and unoaked, minerally Chablis from Burgundy are spot on. In Italy Soave, Orvieto, Verdicchio, Lugana, Fiano, Greco di Tufo, Grillo and northern Pinot Bianco all fit the bill. Greek whites are often brushed with minerality and citrous without being fruity. Many of the 'rediscovered' old white varieties in Europe make this style. You won't often find this style in the New World – winemakers there don't want neutrality in their wines.

11 GREEN, TANGY WHITES

Sharp, grapefruity, lime zesty Sauvignon Blanc from New Zealand, South Africa and Chile lead the way.

Sauvignon Blanc from New Zealand – especially from Marlborough – has tangy, mouthwatering flavours by the bucketful. Chile and South Africa make similar, slightly softer wines as does Spain with Rueda. Sancerre and Pouilly-Fumé from the Loire Valley in France are crisp and refreshing with lighter fruit flavours and a minerally or even a smoky edge. Sauvignon de Touraine offers similar flavours at lower prices. Bordeaux Sauvignon is dry and fresh. The Loire also produces sharp-edged wines from Chenin Blanc, such as Vouvray and white Anjou. Riesling is the other grape to look out for. Rieslings ideally are citrousy, minerally when young, with a streak of green apple and some high tensile acidity. The leanest, often with a touch of scented sweetness to balance the acidity, come from Germany's Mosel Valley; slightly richer ones come from the Rhine; drier, weightier ones from Austria and Alsace. Australian Rieslings, particularly from the Clare and Eden Valleys, start bone dry and age to an irresistible limes-and-toast flavour.

12 INTENSE, NUTTY WHITES

Dry yet succulent whites with subtle nut and oatmeal flavours and sometimes the smell of struck matches. These wines are generally oak aged and have a soft edge with a backbone of absolute dryness. White Burgundy sets the style.

The best expression is oak-aged Chardonnay in the form of white Burgundy. This is the wine that earned Chardonnay its renown in the first place and the style is sometimes matched in the best examples from the New World. Italian producers in Tuscany are having a go, too. Top-quality oak-aged Pessac-Léognan from Bordeaux are Sémillon blended with Sauvignon Blanc, giving a creamy, nutty wine with a hint of nectarines. Unoaked Australian Semillon from the Hunter Valley matures to become custardy and rich. The best white Rioja from Spain, too, becomes nutty and lush with time.

13 RIPE, TOASTY WHITES

Upfront flavours of peaches, apricots and tropical fruits with toasty oaky richness – the traditional flavour of Aussie, Californian and Chilean Chardonnay. Modern examples are generally showing more restraint.

This is the flavour of the Chardonnays that shocked and thrilled the world when California and then Australia began making them 30 years ago. They changed our view of what was possible in white wine flavour and style. Since then we have begun to back off a little from such lush flavours and the producers have throttled back a good deal. Many current Californian and Australian examples are relatively restrained. But the high-octane Chardies are still around if you hanker for one. If you ferment Viognier in new oak it also gives toasty, exotic results. Sémillon in oak becomes mouthfilling and creamy, and barrel-fermented South African Chenin can be quite a mouthful.

14 AROMATIC WHITES

Perfumy wines with exotic and floral fragrances – Gewürztraminer gets my vote for scent, Viognier and Muscat for exotic fruit.

Gewurztraminer from Alsace is packed solid with roses and lychees, face cream and a whole kitchen spice cupboard. No, it's not subtle, but with spicy food, especially Chinese, it can be wonderful. German versions are more floral, and the Italians make their Traminer more toned down. But Slovenia, Slovakia, Croatia and the Czech Republic have a go, and New Zealand Gewürztraminer is a delight. Dry Muscat from Alsace is floral with a heady, hothouse grape scent. Southern France and Spain make less scented styles, and you can

get delicate floral Muscats in northern Italy. Viognier, at its apricots-and-spring flowers best in Condrieu, in the northern Rhône Valley, is planted in the south of France, California and Australia as well; and Godello from north-west Spain is also apricotty, but crisper. Irsai Olivér from Hungary, Torrontés from Argentina and Malagousia from Greece are heady and perfumed. Bacchus in England has a haunting aroma of fresh elderflower.

15 SPARKLING WINES

Bubbles are there to make you happy. Smile, you're drinking fun, not just wine. But good bubbly can have delicious flavours as well.

Champagne sets the standard. Good Champagne has a nutty, bready aroma, appley freshness and fine bubbles. Sparkling wine from Australia, California and New Zealand is made in the same way and it's often just as good and usually cheaper. England is also proving naturally suited to growing grapes for top-quality sparkling wine. Other good French fizzes are Crémant de Bourgogne, Crémant d'Alsace, sparkling Saumur and Blanquette de Limoux from the south. Italian sparklers made from Chardonnay and Pinot Noir are in the Champagne style, but light,

fruity Prosecco and sweet, grapy Asti can be more fun. The best Lambrusco is red, snappy and refreshingly sharp. Spanish Cava can be quite classy and good value. German Sekt, when made from Riesling can be lean, sharp and refreshing. Australian sparkling red wines are wild things all about fun and frolics rather than flavour.

16 RICH, SWEET WHITES

Luscious mouthfuls with intense flavours of peach, pineapple and honey.

In France the sweet wines of Bordeaux are at their gorgeous best in Sauternes and Barsac. These are rich and syrupy wines with intense flavours of peaches and pineapples, barley sugar, butterscotch and honey, all balanced by acidity, and they can age for 20 years or more. Monbazillac, Cérons, Loupiac and Ste-Croix-du-Mont are happy hunting grounds for cheaper, lighter versions. California, New Zealand and Australia have a few intensely rich wines in this style, too. The Loire Valley produces honey- and quince-flavoured sweet wines. Quarts de Chaume, Bonnezeaux, Coteaux du Layon and Vouvray are the wines to look for. Only a few Vouvrays are sweet: they're labelled as *moelleux* or *liquoreux*. Alsace Sélection de Grains Nobles sweeties are rich and unctuous. The sweet wines of Germany have a language all of their own. Beerenauslese and Trockenbeerenauslese are intensely sweet and extremely expensive. The best are made from Riesling: its piercing acidity keeps the sweetness from being overpowering. Austria's sweet wines are similar in style to Germany's, but tend to be weightier. There's also a rarity called Eiswein made from frozen grapes picked in the depths of winter. Canadian icewine is made in the same way, and China has made some. Hungary's Tokaji has a wonderful sweet-sour smoky flavour. Moscatel de Valencia from Spain is a simplehearted splash of rich, grapey fruit.

17 WARMING, FORTIFIED WINES

Sweet wines tasting of raisins and brown sugar, plum and blackberry syrup, and able to take on board all kinds of other scents or flavours as they age – port, madeira and sweet brown sherry are the classics.

Port, the rich red fortified wine of Portugal's Douro Valley, is the classic dark sweet wine. The Portuguese island of Madeira produces some of the most fascinating warming fortifieds, with rich brown smoky flavours and a startling acid bite: Bual and Malmsey are the sweet ones to look out for. Spain produces Oloroso dulce, a rare and delicious sherry with stunning, concentrated flavours and black-brown intensely sweet Pedro Ximenez (or PX). Australian Rutherglen Muscat is astonishingly rich and dark. The fortified Marsala of Sicily and Moscato di Pantelleria are good wines, as rich as brown sugar, with a refreshing shiver of acidity.

18 TANGY, FORTIFIED WINES

Bone dry with startling, stark, almost sour and nutty flavours – this is the true, dry sherry from Andalucia in southern Spain.

Fino is pale in colour, very dry with a thrilling tang. Manzanilla can seem even drier and has a wonderful sourdough perfume and tingling acidity. Amontillado is dry, chestnut-coloured and nutty. Dry oloroso adds deep, burnt flavours. Montilla-Moriles is the neighbouring region to Jerez and produces similar wines. The driest style of Madeira, Sercial, is tangy, steely and savoury; Verdelho is a bit fuller and fatter. Australia and South Africa make excellent sherry-style wines, though without the tang of top-class Spanish fino or manzanilla.

TASTE OF THE GRAPE

The taste of the wine is intimately bound up with the grape variety. Here are some of the classic flavours.

RED
- » **Barbera** A snappy, refreshing Italian red.
- » **Cabernet Franc** Medium, blackcurrant, grassy.
- » **Cabernet Sauvignon** Tannic, blackcurrant, cedar, mint.
- » **Carmenère** Dark, blackcurrant- and pepper-flavoured.
- » **Grenache** Ripe strawberry and spice, often in a blend.
- » **Malbec** Full, lush, plummy scented from Argentina.
- » **Merlot** Juicy and plummy: part of the red Bordeaux blend. Blackcurrant, honey, raisins, mint, plum.
- » **Nebbiolo** Dark, very tannic and difficult to appreciate, prunes, raisins, tobacco, tar, hung game, chocolate.
- » **Pinot Noir** Middleweight, fragrant, often delicate, strawberry, cherry, plum. Silky texture.
- » **Pinotage** Love-hate sturdy, smoky, mulberry and marshmallow-flavoured red from South Africa.
- » **Sangiovese** Medium to full, tobacco, cherry stone, herbs, sometimes vegetal, often chewy, raisins. The mainstay of Tuscan reds.
- » **Syrah/Shiraz** Spicy and warm-hearted. Dark, tannic, savage sometimes, raspberry, blackcurrant, blackberry, plum, herbs, pepper, chocolate, smoke.
- » **Tempranillo** Light to medium, strawberry, vanilla, sometimes blackcurrant, pepper.
- » **Zinfandel** In California, spicy, dark, bramble and pepper flavours.

WHITE
- » **Chardonnay** The classic all-purpose international grape. Dry white, from light, appley and acid to full yeast, butter, cream, hazelnuts, oatmeal, toast.
- » **Chenin Blanc** Very dry to sweet, green apples, lemon, nuts, chalk, to apricots, peach, honey, quince.
- » **Gewürztraminer** Fairly dry to sweet, above all spice, tropical fruit and cosmetic perfume. Best in Alsace.
- » **Muscat** Dry to very sweet, above all grapes, peppery yeast, eating apples to deep orange peel, treacle, raisins and toffee.
- » **Pinot Gris** Neutral in Italy (as in Pinot Grigio). Rich in Alsace, with a hint of honey, and pears in New Zealand.
- » **Riesling** Very dry to very sweet, steely, slate, apple to lime, petrol, raisins, even honey and tropical fruits.
- » **Sauvignon Blanc** Very dry to sweet, green flavours, grapefruit, capsicum, nettles, gooseberry, asparagus, lime zest and elderflower.
- » **Viognier** Full dry, apricot, may blossom, sour cream.

Reading the Label

THE FRONT LABEL varies with the type of wine and from country to country, but it should tell you all the necessary information about the wine. There are now all kinds of labels around the world giving you all the information you need, far more than you need, or in some cases none at all. Here are a few fairly classic examples.

EUROPEAN WINE LABELS

The French appellation system is the most widely known system of quality control for wine in Europe. Other European countries have roughly equivalent gradings, though some have more categories. Quality within any of the levels is not consistent and a good example of a simple wine will be better than a poorly made wine that has barely complied with the Appellation rules.

BORDEAUX

1. **Classification** This tells you that the wine was included in the famous 1855 Classification of the red wines of Bordeaux.
2. **Traditional imagery** for a traditional Bordeaux producer. The vast majority of Bordeaux labels still feature a straightforward illustration of the château building. Any that do not are probably making a statement about their modern approach.
3. **Château name** Any wine estate in France, especially in Bordeaux, can take a château name, regardless of whether it has a grand building. Castello is the equivalent word in Italy, Castillo in Spain and Schloss in Germany.
4. **Appellation** European wine regulations expect the appellation name to tell you all you need to know about the origin of the wine, its quality classification and the grape varieties used. But they often presume you have knowledge you don't possess. St-Estèphe in Bordeaux is best known for its slow-maturing, tannic red wines based on Cabernet Sauvignon.
5. **Vintage** The year the grapes were harvested. In most parts of the world the year's weather influences the style of wine, its ripeness, alcohol level and longevity. It's also important to check the vintage to see whether the wine is ready to drink.

BURGUNDY

1. **Domaine bottling** This means that the wine was bottled on the estate. Anything not bottled 'à la propriété' or 'au domaine' is most likely a less distinguished offering from a large merchant or co-operative.
2. **Grand Cru** This is the top level of the Burgundy classification. Montrachet is the name of a famous Grand Cru and as such does not need to include the name of its village on the label.
3. **Name of the producer**, in this case a leading Burgundy estate. 'Domaine' means wine estate and is commonly used in Burgundy rather than château.

WINE LABELS OUTSIDE EUROPE

Labels from wine regions outside Europe are usually clearly laid out and easy to understand.

CLOUDY BAY

1. **Name of the producer** Wines produced outside the traditional appellation areas of Europe often promote the producer name over that of any region.
2. **Iconic design** A simple graphic image is commonly used for wine labels outside Europe, in the same way as a European coat of arms. The Cloudy Bay brand has become instantly recognizable because of the strong image.
3. **Grape variety** The name of the grape is more important on this label than any region (Marlborough in New Zealand). Cloudy Bay has become such an iconic wine that you don't even need to put on the name of the region. The grape variety is enough.
4. **Vintage** The year the grapes were harvested. Knowing how old the wine is will give you an idea of whether it will taste young or mature. Wines from the southern hemisphere go on sale in the autumn of the same year as the harvest.

ANATOMY OF A BOTTLE

1. **Closures** can be screwcap, as here (consistent and inert so the wine is reliable every time) or the more traditional cork, from the bark of cork trees chiefly found in Portugal and around the edges of the Mediterranean. It is the most efficient form of closure for wines requiring aging and the minute interchange of air which develops character. Plastic corks are OK for early-drinking wines.
2. **Capsule** used with a cork. Traditionally made of lead, but now tin-foil or plastic, it acts to keep the cork clean, stop insects like cork weevil eating it, and help maintain moisture, stopping the cork drying out.
3. **Ullage** This is the gap between the closure and the wine. You want as small a gap as possible, because a large gap will show that the wine has begun to seep through the cork; since it will be replaced by air at a faster rate, decay will set in. Older wines have naturally more 'ullage' because the cork will eventually shrink. In general, try to choose a wine with as little ullage as possible.
4. **Neck label** Some bottles have a neck label which usually shows the vintage date and maybe the shipper's name.
5. **Shoulder** This bottle is a typical Bordeaux shape with high shoulders. Burgundy bottles have sloping shoulders.
6. **Label** This should tell you all the necessary information concerning the wine. It varies with the type of wine and from country to country. There may also be a back label with additional information.
7. **Punt** This indentation in the bottom of the bottle is to catch sediment. Since few cheap wines have sediment, many of them are in bottles without punts.

The World of Wine

A sense of place may be the most precious, the most coveted character that a wine can possess. But can you smell it? Can you taste it? Can you feel it as you roll the wine across your tongue?

Sometimes you are sure that you can. Sometimes you are sure that the rich blackberry fruit you taste is streaked with a mineral fire and scratched with a smell of heat and hillside that could only come from the herb-strewn, sun-scorched vineyard you visited, and where you bought the wine. Sometimes you are sure that the dancing acidity, the gossamer daintiness and the cut of slate in a Mosel Riesling; or the dark, dry, imperious, gruff but not unfriendly fruit, rattled and rubbed by the undertow of stones and gravel, that you recognise in a brooding Bordeaux red – you are sure that these feel exactly 'of their place'. And there are other wines, of less perfume, of less flavour, of less texture and presence, that still manage to tell you something of the grapes that gave them life. Not all vineyards are noble, beautiful, blessed by nature. Not all grape varieties are packed with personality, seductive or witty, cerebral, or swooning with scent. But if the winemakers are honest, if the grapes are grown well, and the wine is made with no attempt to be what it is not, then these wines also have a sense of place. We have all drunk a pitcher of basic red or pink or white that was just the perfect expression of the place where we were, the perfect flavour and texture. At that moment, with that meal, among those friends, it was the perfect wine. And no other wine, no more sophisticated or expensive offering, could have given us such a 'sense of place'.

Well, in this book I have tried to reveal the sense of place for as many wines as I can. I talk about wines great and small, about flavours memorable and fleeting. But, above all, I try to lead you into this wonderful world of wine that is my World of Wine.

The village of Piesport huddles on the banks of the river Mosel, beneath a great south-facing wall of vines that manages to capture every last ray of summer sun to help the Riesling grapes ripen to perfect ripeness. You can understand at a glance why grapes can ripen here in such a northerly region – the vines are almost at the water's edge to benefit from the reflected light and heat from the river, and the forests on top of the hillside protect the vineyards from the winds. These wines can be fragile, pale and an ethereal 7.5 per cent of alcohol, or dripping with honey and peach sweetness if picked very late in a warm year.